BIOGRAPHIES OF DIVERSE HEROES

SONIA SOTOMAYOR

STEPHANIE GASTON

TABLE OF CONTENTS

A Crabtree Seedlings Book

CRABTREE
Publishing Company
www.crabtreebooks.com

School-to-Home Support for Caregivers and Teachers

This book helps children grow by letting them practice reading. Here are a few guiding questions to help the reader with building his or her comprehension skills. Possible answers appear here in red.

Before Reading:

- What do I think this book is about?
  - *I think this book is about a real person named Sonia Sotomayor.*
  - *I think this book is about Sonia Sotomayor's experiences as a judge.*

- What do I want to learn about this topic?
  - *I want to learn how many women have served on the Supreme Court.*
  - *I want to learn if Sonia Sotomayor was a lawyer before she became a judge.*

During Reading:

- I wonder why...
  - *I wonder why Sonia Sotomayor wanted to become a lawyer.*
  - *I wonder why Sonia Sotomayor only worked for a few years as a trial lawyer before becoming a corporate lawyer.*

- What have I learned so far?
  - *I have learned that Sonia Sotomayor is the first Hispanic to serve on the Supreme Court.*
  - *I have learned that Sonia Sotomayor was also a law professor at Columbia Law School.*

After Reading:

- What details did I learn about this topic?
  - *I have learned that in May 2009, Sonia Sotomayor was nominated to the Supreme Court.*
  - *I have learned that Sonia Sotomayor has written several children's books.*

- Read the book again and look for the glossary words.
  - *I see the word* ***Hispanic*** *on page 4 and the word* ***professor*** *on page 14. The other glossary words are found on page 22.*

SONIA SOTOMAYOR

Sonia Sotomayor is a member of the **Supreme Court** of the United States.

Sotomayor is the first **Hispanic** to serve on the Supreme Court.

Five women have served on the Supreme Court. Pictured here in 2010 are four of them: Sandra Day O'Connor, Sonia Sotomayor, Ruth Bader Ginsburg, and Elena Kagan.

She is also the third woman to serve on the Supreme Court.

Sotomayor was born in New York City on June 25, 1954.

Her family is from Puerto Rico.

Sotomayor graduated high school with top honors.

She attended Princeton University, and then Yale Law School.

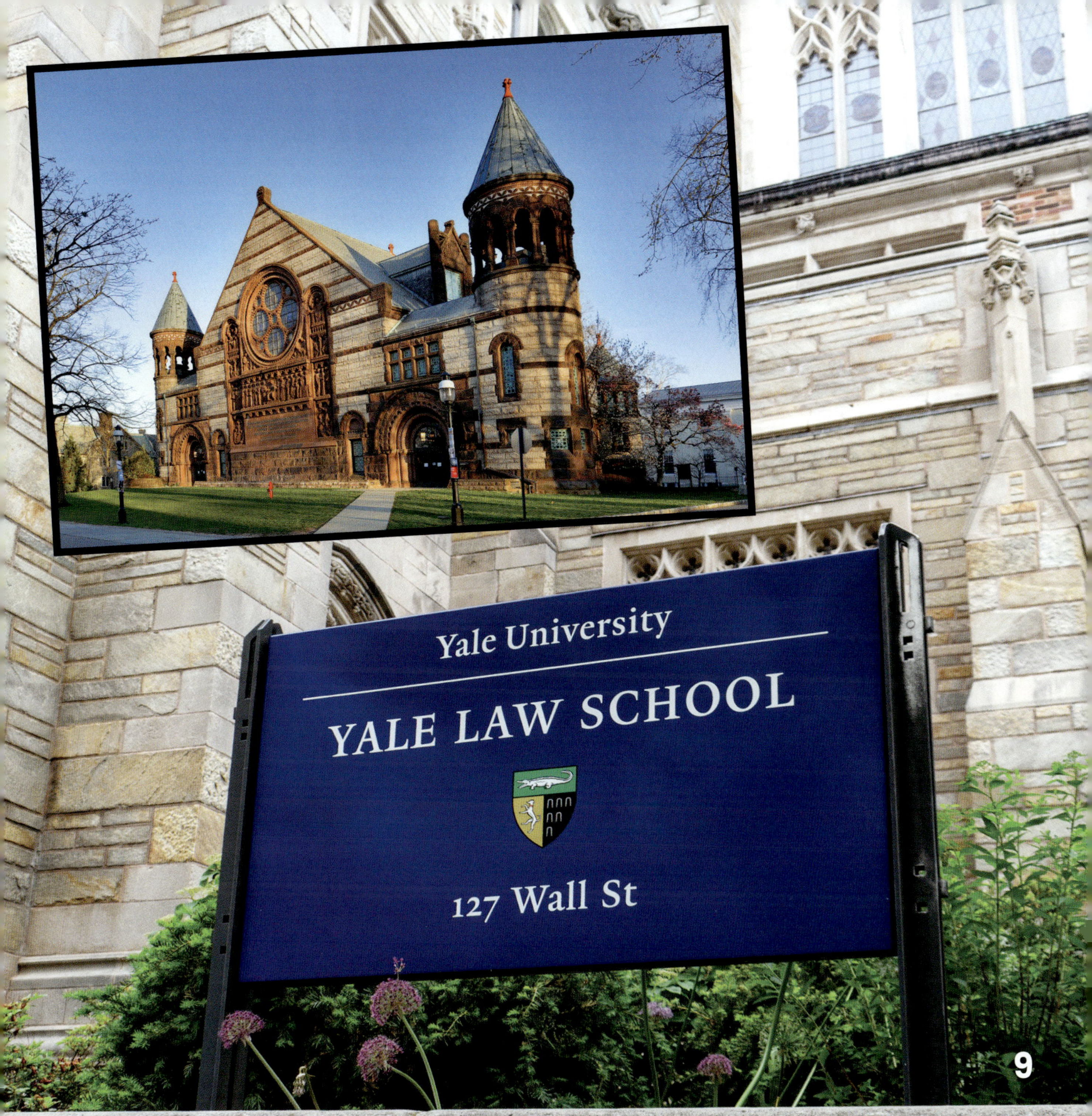
Yale University
YALE LAW SCHOOL
127 Wall St

In 1980, Sotomayor began working as a trial lawyer in New York.

A few years later, she became a **corporate** lawyer.

In 1991, Sotomayor was **nominated** to the United States District Court.

She would hear more than 3,000 cases as a judge.

Sotomayor was also a law **professor**.

She taught at New York University and Columbia Law School.

NYU
NYUStudentServices
SHAFTWA
SHAFTW

Sotomayor served as a judge on the Court of Appeals from 1998 to 2009.

And in May 2009, Sotomayor was nominated to the Supreme Court.

Sotomayor was nominated by three U.S. presidents over her career.

George H. W. Bush

Bill Clinton

Barack Obama

She has been among the majority vote in **landmark** cases.

In 2013, Sotomayor released a book about her life called *My Beloved World*.

Sotomayor has also written several children's books.

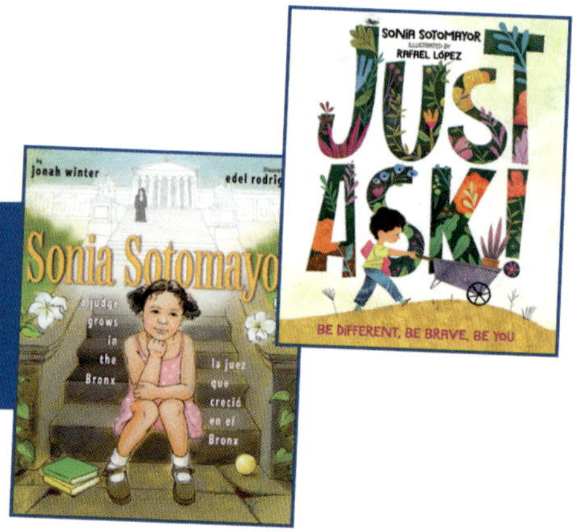

Sonia
Sotomayor
My Beloved
World

Glossary

corporate (kawr-prit): Relating to large companies or a particular large company

Hispanic (hi-span-ik): Relating to Spanish-speaking countries, especially those of Latin America

landmark (land-mahrk): An important event that creates lasting change

nominated (nom-uh-neyt-id): To be officially named as someone in the running during an election

professor (pruh-fes-er): A teacher of the highest rank in a college or university

Supreme Court (suh-preem kawrt): The highest court in a country or state

Index

"My job as a prosecutor is to do justice. And justice is served when a guilty man is convicted and an innocent man is not."

—Sonia Sotomayor

About the Author

Stephanie Gaston is a content producer for CNN and a screenwriter. She spent more than a decade working for the FOX and ABC affiliates in Miami, Florida, before joining the ranks at CNN in 2015, ahead of an unprecedented election cycle. Stephanie is a first-generation Haitian American who grew up in Fort Lauderdale, Florida, a diverse community with Latin and Caribbean influences. Throughout her career in journalism, Stephanie has covered major stories including presidential inaugurations, natural disasters, and royal weddings. Stephanie is a dog lover, movie buff, fitness enthusiast, and most importantly, a proud mom.

CRABTREE
Publishing Company

Written by: Stephanie Gaston
Designed by: Under the Oaks Media
Proofreader: Petrice Custance
Print coordinator: Katherine Berti

Photographs: Steve Pettway: cover, p. 5, 19; Fred Schilling: p. 3; LOC: p. 6, 13; Rainer Lesniewski; GM/Current Affairs: p. 8; Jay Yuan: p. 9 (top); Michael Vi: p. 9; Nirat.pic: p. 10-11; littlenystock: p. 15; Felix Lipov: p. 16; K2Images: p. 17; Pete Souza: p. 18; Everett Collection: p. 21

Library and Archives Canada Cataloguing in Publication

Available at the Library and Archives Canada

Library of Congress Cataloging-in-Publication Data

Available at the Library of Congress

Crabtree Publishing Company

www.crabtreebooks.com 1-800-387-7650

In Canada: We acknowledge the financial support of the Government of Canada through the Canada Book Fund for our publishing activities.

Published in the United States
Crabtree Publishing
347 Fifth Avenue
Suite 1402-145
New York, NY, 10016

Published in Canada
Crabtree Publishing
616 Welland Ave.
St. Catharines, ON
L2M 5V6

Printed in the U.S.A./072022/CG20220201